THE NEWBORN *Mama*

ASHLEY TOBIN

SKRYBE

Published by Skrybe Ltd.

Contents

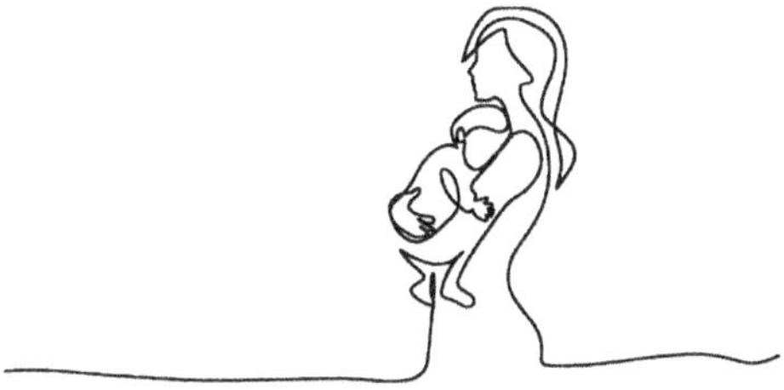

The moment a child is born,
the mother is also born.

She never existed before. The
woman existed, but the
mother, never.

A mother is something
absolutely new.

– Bhagwan Shree Rajneesh

Welcome to Motherhood

Introduction

Congratulations, Mama– you did it! You stretched, you grew, you nourished, and you made a new life happen. Now that Baby is out of your belly and in your arms, the fun really begins. You're bound to feel a wide range of emotions, and you're going to have a lot of changes in the early weeks and months as you navigate life as a new mom.

Caring for a newborn is a learning curve, and along it, we hope this book serves as a comfort and support – as well as a guide to caring for yourself while doing so for Baby. You'll lose sleep but gain confidence; take a break from some of your favorite activities but find you enjoy them even more than ever once you return; lose touch with people who don't serve you and deepen bonds with those who show up.

Everyone is going to have an opinion about how you raise this child, but from day one we want you to feel empowered to make those choices as they best fit you and your baby. From feeding options to your social life, to sleep and clutter tips, and how to rediscover the woman you were before Baby, we'll be there to help you navigate the newborn stage like the pro you are already becoming.

As you forge a new path in your identity as a mama, we hope to put some tools in your belt that will ease the transition and create space in your day for mindfulness, calm, and self-care. With journal prompts and easy meditation ideas, quick-read advice from seasoned parents, resources, and therapeutic techniques to get your emotions in check, let this book fill the role of an experienced and loving best friend who just happens to hang out on your nightstand or in your diaper bag for a quick pick-me-up at any time.

As you start any given morning or close out the day with a new chapter or by rereading one you need again, just remember that you are not alone on this tumultuous and rewarding path. Most importantly – you are the best mama for that sweet little baby, and you deserve to give yourself as much love as you do them.

An Emotional Rollercoaster

Tackling the Highs and Lows

This is it—your moment has arrived. You are now a mama and the whole world has changed. While nurses, family, friends, and even strangers in the grocery store are cooing and gushing over Baby, it's important for you to also take this time to take care of *you*. The journey to motherhood may have been long and winding, but now that you're here, things will be less straight and predictable than ever before. But with time you will feel less overwhelmed and gain your stride. Like any big life change, an adjustment period is necessary, and this is by far one of the biggest life changes there is, so be easy on yourself and take it one day at a time.

It all starts with a deep breath and the reminder that you matter just as much as your baby does. Your joy, your rest, your nutrition, and your fulfillment are just as important now as they were before you were responsible for the care of another life, if not even more so. Be kind to yourself as you embark on the days, weeks, and months ahead. Your baby will benefit from a mother who is calm, rested, and OK.

A Range of Emotions

Let's talk about feelings for a moment. You've likely anticipated the moment that little baby will be placed in your arms for months—or even long before actually planning a family. And when thinking about this special time, we usually expect to feel nothing but sheer joy and elation at the sight of our brand-new baby.

But in case no one has told you this yet, a full range of emotions is normal. Exhaustion, stress, the physical discomfort of recovery, a fluctuation of hormones, and many other factors can contribute to a mind that feels suddenly filled with more than just joy. The dopamine rush that comes on strong right after Baby is born is one of the most incredible highs of any mom's life. Yet, by Day Two, many mothers report a slew of tears, a listless feeling, and the onset of worries and sadness.

I'll never forget the second night of my first daughter's life when I found myself crying constantly without being able to pinpoint why. A kind nurse listened as I told her I was so happy but also so sad and a bit confused; I was scared at not understanding these feelings and felt so relieved when she said, "Oh, honey, this is just what Day Two is like!" Learning that what I was experiencing was a very normal hormonal reaction that happens on the second day of life put me at ease and helped me to get through it.

When my subsequent babies were born and that familiar swell of tears cropped up on the second day, I was comforted by the reminder that Day Two can be like that. And don't be alarmed if it happens again on any random day in the weeks to come—your hormones are all over the place and so, too, will your feelings be.

It is also completely normal—and rarely discussed—that not every mother feels instantly bonded to her baby. Try to be easy on yourself and lean on your birthing team, partner, and any family or friends that have offered to help. Soon, things will take a turn. In the first few weeks or even months of the baby's life, bonding can happen slowly as you and your baby get to know each other. A delay in these feelings doesn't make you any less of a wonderful mother; you've undergone a huge event physically and emotionally, and everyone heals differently.

Sheer exhaustion can also affect those bonding feelings. Of course you love your baby; but if it takes a while to fall *in love* with them, that doesn't mean anything is wrong with you. Cuddling and holding them, bonding at feeding time, and taking walks outside when the weather agrees will all help. But in addition to physical bonding time, you might find that some away time helps, too. Let someone else watch Baby while you take a nap or run an errand alone from time to time. Getting rest and small reminders of who you were before can help immensely while you adjust.

A Changed Body

On the topic of healing, look at what your body is capable of! How incredible is it that you grew an entire human inside, and guided it earthside with your boundless strength? Whether you delivered vaginally or via C-section, you are an absolute warrior, and your body will show the evidence of that for some time.

If you're feeling weepy or defeated about stretch marks, weight gain, and other physical signs of pregnancy and birth, this can contribute to a low mood. There are ways to combat these feelings, and it all comes down to taking care of yourself. Don't rush to lose the baby weight by forcing exercise or limiting calorie intake; it took nine months to gain the weight, and losing it doesn't happen overnight.

Instead, wear clothes that are comfortable and fit well. Eat food that nourishes you and gives you energy. Surround yourself with people who are supportive, loving, and remind you how beautiful you are. And don't forget to get in pictures with your baby, not just take snaps of them. One day you'll look back on this time and want to see yourself with them, even if right now you feel shy and sensitive about your physical appearance. As you continue to heal, you'll feel better and better about yourself. Trust the process and remember to thank your body for the ways it stretched and grew to accommodate this new life. Gentle yoga and meditation can help, and staying hydrated will be beneficial physically and emotionally.

Observing & Handling Your Emotions

There's a philosophy many cognitive behavioral therapists use wherein tough emotions are not ignored or overridden, but also not delved into or allowed to fester and bring us down. Instead, they are *observed.*

Close your eyes, or keep them open, and fix them on something stationary in the room. Clear your mind as best you can and let the thoughts and feelings arise as they will. The exercise here, as Amy Wapner, MS, ADTR, a therapist from New York City, explains, is to *notice* the feelings rather than go careening down a path with them:

It is important that we remain aware of our emotions, and notice them as they pass through us, without holding them so tightly they define or constrict us, and we also allow them to pass by as we notice, "Oh yes, there is the sadness." In doing so, we can allow ourselves not to overly identify with an emotion and yet not be in denial of its existence. This way, we strive to be emotionally "clean."

Leaning on Your Support System

Now is not the time to try and be a hero and do it all yourself. Let the people around you who want to help, help. Your partner or friends, your parents or neighbors, your healthcare professionals. Sometimes the simple act of accepting a home-cooked meal from a member of your community can be all it takes to bring your anxiety down a notch. One less thing for you to do!

Don't be ashamed of hiring some help, either. A part-time cleaner, occasional laundry person, or any other way you can delegate some of the chores will take a huge load off of you and free you up to rest and relax while the baby is sleeping. You might also consider a night nurse, a mother's helper, or just a couple hours of afternoon babysitting every once in a while so you can rest. Many moms are amazed at how much better they feel when they've just had a bit of rest and/or time to themselves.

What worked for my little family with the addition of each new baby was for my partner to take even an hour off of me. Never a napper before, I found the exhaustion of caring for a newborn rendered me newly able to fall asleep at a moment's notice. When our first baby was very young, my husband would take her on long walks in the stroller in the early morning before work so I could sleep in. With our second, what worked best was for him to get home a bit early and take Baby from me in the late afternoon while I napped alongside our toddler and woke up refreshed for dinner.

You'll find your stride and figure out what works best for you; just know it is absolutely normal to need and want a break, and try to take one when you can. Your tough emotions will feel much more manageable when your sleep bank is fuller.

Reducing Your Workload

Another way to combat a low mood is by unburdening yourself of some of the tasks before you. When you've been taking care of a new baby all day (and night!) and trying to take care of yourself as well, sometimes taking care of the house too can just feel like way too much. Try to take it easy on yourself with household chores or delegate them to others living in the home.

If you are struggling with feeling like the home is in chaos and that makes you feel more anxious or sad, try the two-room hack. This is a process that allows you to relax in a tidied-up environment without spending hours cleaning. Dedicate one day-time space (like the living room or lounge) and one night-time space (your bedroom or Baby's), and remove or hide any excess clutter from the room. Enjoy these two spaces stress-free while you are healing inside and out, and worry about the rest of the house later.

During this time, do not feel guilty about eating takeout, using disposable plates, or whatever else you have to do to unburden yourself. Baby's needs are straightforward if relentless; yours are a bit more nuanced but just as important.

Grieving the Loss of Your Old Lifestyle

Adjusting to the new baby can bring up reminders of everything you aren't doing now. Especially in those first several weeks, caring for an infant is an around-the-clock job and leaves no time for your old interests or lifestyle. It is normal to be saddened by those losses, but just know it won't be forever. Babies grow more quickly than you can comprehend right now; feeding windows lengthen; independence blooms; and you'll be back in the world soon.

Don't forget that your old self is still in there; she's just taking a brief break. Coffee shops and yoga classes, work and friends, travel, and whatever else you love will be a part of your life again before you know it. It's OK to not fully enjoy the moment that you're in or to feel frustrated by milk-soaked shirts, piles of laundry, and waking up every other hour all night long. This is *hard.* But it will pass and improve; just give it time and be gentle with yourself. Remember that billions of mothers throughout history have been in your exact position and that their lives weren't like this for long.

Baby Blues or Depression?

The "baby blues" are a cute term for a not-so-cute phenomenon. They can happen to anyone, but they do not affect everyone. The baby blues are a temporary state of depression caused by hormonal shifts right after birth that typically resolve on their own within two weeks. If you're experiencing the baby blues, you might find yourself crying excessively and feeling down, hopeless, and anxious during the first couple of weeks after Baby's birth.

Other symptoms of the baby blues include temporary sleeplessness, appetite loss, mood swings, and a feeling of edginess. Many of these mirror depression and may be scary to a new mom, especially someone who has never experienced mental health struggles before. However, the baby blues are a temporary state that should only last the first several days, up to two weeks or so.

Severe or debilitating feelings of depression or anxiety, or a lingering state of perpetual sadness or worry, could be more than the baby blues. If you've passed the two-week mark and feel a disinterest in caring for yourself or Baby, are scared to leave the house, cannot stop crying even when rested, or feel otherwise down and sad with no resolution, you may be suffering from postpartum depression and/or anxiety.

When (& How) to Seek Help

PPD/PPA affects anywhere up to 20% of new mothers, so this is nothing rare and certainly not your fault. If you think you may be suffering from postpartum anxiety and/or depression, there is a world of mental healthcare options available to you. Getting past PPD and PPA with the help of a professional will return to you the joy of motherhood that you so deserve and is a key part of the care you need.

If you are comfortable discussing the suspicion of PPD/PPA with your primary care physician or prenatal team, they can often help directly or set you up with the right doctors and recommend a great therapist to help. Help comes in many forms, including talk therapy, cognitive behavioral strategies, and, in some cases, temporary medication regimens if you and your doctor agree on that route.

If you don't have a doctor you trust to discuss your worries with, there are free and accessible resources available to you. In the US, contact the National Maternal Health Hotline at 1-833-TLC-MAMA (1-833-852-6262) for assistance. In the UK, there is Pre and Postnatal Depression Advice and Support (PANDAS) – helpline at 0808 196 1776 (11am to 10pm every day) or email info@pandasfoundation.or g.uk and the Association for Post Natal Illness is available via phone at 020 7386 0868 (10am to 2pm, Monday to Friday) or by email at info@apni.org.

There is also an international support hotline for mothers everywhere experiencing symptoms of PPD. You can always call the Postpartum Support International helpline at 800-944-4773 for support, resources, information, and to be connected with physicians and support groups in your area.

Emotional Breaks

Mindfulness can be tough to attain when you're feeding an infant around the clock and trying to take care of yourself and your home as well. A positive of the first few weeks of Baby's life is that they sleep a lot, and when they are sleeping—even if that is happening on top of you!—your mind and soul can take some breaks.

Throughout this book, we'll provide prompts for meditation and journaling—things you can spend a minute or five on, without having to sit up straight or focus too hard. Little ways to return your mind toward centering and calm and to eke out a bit of self-care at a time when you need it most.

Take a Mindful Minute

Journal Prompts:

- *Gratitude.* Your body has been through a lot, and looks and feels different right now. Jot down three things you are grateful to your body for; these can be separate body parts at work or how your whole body has functioned and served you this year.

- *Reminder.* The woman you were just days ago is not gone forever. Ruminate on another time in your life when you experienced a change and eventually got back to doing the things you loved (job change, moving houses, illness, or surgeries).

- *Words.* Too tired for sentences? Just try some words. Make a list of the one-word emotions, thoughts, etc. that come to mind in these early days. This may lead to helping you sort through the harder words, and it'll remind you of the positives poking through as well.

Mindfulness Exercise:

With Baby secured safely, carve out as little as 60 seconds or as many minutes as you can spare. Close your eyes and picture a lemon. It sounds random, but the shape, color, and citrusy-clean association the mind receives from the image of lemon is a great way to cleanse the mental palette. Breathe in through your nose and out through your mouth, holding the breath at "the top" between the inhale and exhale.

Tense the muscles in your face all at once, and then release them. Do the same with the neck and shoulders, followed by arms and hands, stomach, and down through your body in succession. This exercise can be done expeditiously, or you can take more time with it if you have it. Allow your mind to wander if it wants to, but don't follow it down those meandering paths. Keeping to the tense-and-release pattern from head to toe, you should feel a wash of calm come over you. When you're finished, it may be a great time to return to the "words" journaling and see if any new ones come up.

Be well, Mama, and take care of yourself in little ways, as often as you possibly can.

Don't stress over your housework, just take each day as it comes and enjoy the cuddles.

A Real Mama

Fed is Best

Breastfeeding, Bottle-feeding & Combi-feeding

Before diving into our chapter on feeding, let's highlight the most important takeaway here: Fed is best. Full stop. A happy baby is the result of a happy mother, one who feels fulfilled, satisfied, and at ease. Breastfeeding is a great choice. Bottle-feeding is a great choice. A combination of feeding by both breast and bottle is also a great choice.

If breastfeeding does not work out for you, or it's your preference not to do so, your child will be nurtured and nourished and will thrive the same as a breastfed baby. Some breastfed babies require extra calories outside of the standard amount they take in from Mama at the breast for the first few weeks or months. Some babies don't tolerate their mother's milk. Some mothers thoroughly enjoy breastfeeding, and their babies agree.

Whatever your feeding journey entails, it is your own and your baby's. It is no one else's place to weigh in and push the bottle or breast on you. If Baby is making diapers and gaining weight, carry on as you are. If you have fears that they are not receiving enough nutrition, your pediatrician or baby nurse can do a weighted feed and give you strategies on getting their calories up on a case-by-case basis.

However you choose to feed Baby, to follow are all our top tips.

Breastfeeding Tips

Nursing comes naturally for some women and their babies, but not for most. It will take a day or two, or longer, for your milk to come in fully. In the first 48 hours and beyond, you might feel like Baby is on the breast at all times. Skin-to-skin and frequent latching can be tiring but will help your milk come in. Until it does, Baby is ingesting nature's power food—the nutrient-rich, yellow newborn food known as colostrum. A newborn's stomach is tiny (about the size of an almond on Day One and a ping-pong ball by Day Ten), so they do not need a lot to be full. If breastfeeding is your route and Baby is at the breast often in those early days, don't worry that they are not getting enough. Colostrum will be enough to sate them until your milk arrives in full force.

Your trusted pediatrician or lactation consultant is the best person to give you advice on how often to feed your baby and an exact plan depending on their needs. Typically, once your milk is in, you should aim to start each new feed at the two-hour mark from the start of the last feed. Since newborn babies often fall asleep at the breast and can take a while to get in a full feed, this process can leave you feeling like you're always nursing.

We promise, it won't be like this forever! You might consider a pacifier between feeds to give Baby something for soothing and rest that allows you (and your nipples!) a break.

Breastfeeding & Pain

Speaking of your nipples, they are going to take some time to adjust to this new lifestyle. Soreness and cracking are normal, and pain with breastfeeding does not necessarily mean you are having problems in this area. If you suspect a lip or tongue tie, don't hesitate to get Baby checked for one, but many occurrences of breast pain are very normal and will pass soon.

Our nipples are sensitive and not used to being wet and pulled on all day; chapping, just like what happens to our lips and hands, is possible. Nipple balms and gel patches can be a source of great relief. Nipple shields are another hack moms have been using for ages that are comfortable, help pull out an inverted nipple, which aids in some latch issues, and also prevent chafing and reduce pain.

They also make vented plastic shells that can be tucked inside your bra to hold fabric away from the nipples and promote air flow to soothe and protect them. The first time a nurse pulled a set of these out of their plastic wrap and shoved them down my top, I nearly wept with relief. In time, your nipples will toughen up, and the pain and chapping will fade. Promise!

Some moms also experience a degree of pain with milk letdown, which, again, is normal. Ditto the pain that can come from a surge in milk production between feeds. Pumping a little to relieve pressure and massaging the area, especially in the shower, can help.

Nourishing Your Baby & Yourself

"Cluster feeding," when Baby seems to be taking in multiple feeds back-to-back or wants to be at the breast nearly constantly, is normal in stretches during the first several weeks and can happen again at key growth points in the months ahead. Set yourself up for success by creating a comfortable space to feed the baby while keeping everything you need on hand. Avoid feeling "trapped" by setting up a little station (some moms use a little wheeled cart, but any small bin or basket will do). Keep this stocked with snacks, a bottle of water, the TV remote, books and magazines, a phone charger, and whatever else will help the time pass to avoid stress and frustration during endless feeds.

About those snacks: Now is not the time to worry about cutting calories to lose weight. Nursing mothers burn about 500–700 calories a day, especially in the early months, and your body needs extra fuel to accommodate this. Oat or granola bars, peanut butter and crackers, fruit, nuts, cheese sticks (non-dairy if Baby has a milk intolerance), and other nutrient-dense snacks that feel like a mini-meal are all great choices.

If you are not fed enough, your breastfed baby will not be fed enough. Consider it the most selfless thing in the world right now to indulge in the snacks that satisfy, and enjoy a bit of R&R in front of the TV or with a good book in hand during a long feed, or when Baby falls asleep in your arms and you're afraid to move and wake them up.

Just When You Think You've Got it Down...

Even breastfeeding pros will have a story or two to tell you about how tough this gig can be. One mom hilariously recounted for us this mortifying tale of an experience a few months into breast-feeding when she really thought she had it all under control:

> *Once I got over the initial struggles of breastfeeding, I thought it was great and loved how I could just feed when and wherever my little one needed to. What no one told me was that by a certain age, babies like to take a mid-milk break and look around. During one feed at the doctor's, unbeknownst to me, my whole boob was exposed to the entire doctor's waiting room and one very flustered elderly man sitting opposite!*

Just as she's able to look back and laugh now, you will also think back on these early days with humor and compassion for yourself. Like everything else about becoming a mommy, breastfeeding has a learning curve. You're only at the beginning, and you are already doing great!

A Pumping Plan & Breaks for Mom

Whether you decide to set aside time between feeds to pump or are not interested in extra work, there are simple ways to build up a stash of breast milk. This will allow your baby to get used to drinking from a bottle; create an opportunity for them to bond with your partner, parents, and other special people in their life; and give you a much-needed break. Once my eldest was back at birth weight and the pediatrician advised us to let her sleep in longer stretches overnight, I would add a pumping session into my routine in the middle of the night when she slept through a typical feed time. I didn't mind this routine and have fond memories of standing up in the kitchen eating chocolate squares to the whir of my breast pump in peaceful solitude.

By my second baby, that old routine seemed outrageous to me, and I swore to never make myself wake up when the baby wasn't crying for me. Instead, I took a "lazy" approach to breast milk collection that served beautifully; I'd use a silicone suction-on milk collector on one breast to catch the letdown on that side while my baby nursed on the other side. Surprisingly, this simple method helped me build up an impressive freezer stash without ever pumping in the first six months of my daughter's life.

Bottle-Bonding & Benefits

People love to talk about the miracle of Mom's milk, but we also want to remind you of the absolute miracle that is formula. Like breastmilk, formula contains the nutrients needed to help Baby grow and is gentle on their tiny tummies. Bottle-feeding your baby mirrors nursing patterns in that most infants feed often in the early days, but many moms report that their formula-fed babies seem fuller and more content after a feed, allowing longer stretches of sleep.

Bottle-bonding is beautiful. Stare into your little one's sweet eyes while they eat, and remember that you are their sole focus and that they just adore you. Feeding is their favorite part of the day, and while they are in your arms enjoying their food, the two of you are just as close as a breastfeeding mother-baby duo.

Bottle-fed babies are adaptable to various caretakers and won't experience nipple confusion with a pacifier (three cheers for more sleep for all!). And if your little one has any food allergies, it is much easier to eliminate them instantly from their diet when they are fed formula vs. breast milk.

Of course, a key benefit of formula is that it can be helpful, and in many cases, absolutely essential, for the mother's mental health. If the taxing schedule of breastfeeding, low milk production, difficult latch, or other breastfeeding woes prove too hard, resentment and depression can creep in. Giving your body a break and feeding by bottle will not only take those stresses off your shoulders but also give others a chance to feed Baby, carving out more time for you to sleep and take care of yourself. Regardless of how the baby is fed, a mother who has had rest and breaks is what they truly need.

Combination Feeding

It's not often discussed, but combination feeding is a third option that proves successful for many moms. This method involves substituting one or more feeds a day with formula instead of breast milk. You may choose to pump while Baby takes the bottle or just rest. Combination feeding is a great compromise for those who enjoy breastfeeding but crave a break and a chance to let others step in. It is also a nutrition builder for babies who are born early, are tiny, or acting hungry after some nursing sessions.

You'll find your groove as Baby grows, and decide as you go what method of feeding works best for you and your baby.

Support in Feeding

Whether breast or bottle, lean on your partner for help. If you are exclusively nursing, there is a very simple way they can help without doing any actual feeding themselves. Your partner can get up when Baby wakes crying, bring them to you for a feed, and then burp, change, and get them back down so you can go right back to sleep after nursing.

If you pump at all, they can clean your pump parts for you, help organize the refrigerator or freezer stash, and wash and sanitize bottles between feeds. They can also focus on making you nutritious snacks and meals to keep you sated while you produce food for your baby.

Of course, with bottle-feeding, whether those bottles contain breast milk or formula (or both!), your partner should take over some feeds during the day to allow you a break and some time for mental healthcare, sleep, or simple relaxation. The prompts to follow can provide some welcome ways to unwind your mind in the midst of a feeding frenzy.

The Bottom Line

The most important thing we said in this chapter was in the very first paragraph: Fed is best. Your baby and your body are in charge here; don't let anyone tell you how to feed your child. Some meddlers will love to say that you can't produce enough milk and that all moms need to add formula. Other judgers enjoy touting the benefits of breast milk and ignoring those of bottle feeding. At the end of the day (and in the middle of the night!), the only thing that matters is that Baby is being fed and nourished. Turn down the noise from the outside world and feed your baby as only you know best.

Take a Mindful Minute

Journal Prompts:

- Breastfeeding Affirmation: *I am creating all the nourishment my baby needs to thrive.* Follow with a list of the triumphs you've experienced so far on your breastfeeding journey. These can be big things like tracking Baby's weight gain or small things like the sweet look on Baby's milk-drunk face as you write.

- Bottle Affirmation: *My baby is fed and loved, and I provide the nourishment he/she needs.* Journal on the best parts of your feeding day with Baby. The cozy cuddles you enjoy while feeding, getting a stretch of sleep overnight while your partner is on bottle duty, etc.

Mindfulness Exercise:

A fed baby is a growing baby. A growing baby is a healthy baby. If you've been feeling pressure, anxiety, worry, judgment, or any unease related to feeding, this quick positive-thinking exercise can help.

In your mind's eye, look at that tiny baby the moment they emerged from your womb and now. It's only been a brief window of time, but already they are growing. Those spindly legs will soon be chubby, and those beautiful, bright eyes will be open for more of the day. Flaky newborn skin gains moisture and stays intact. Sweet little fingers unclench. *You* are the one who is guiding your baby on this journey. Never doubt for a moment that you are doing the best for your baby, no matter how you feed them.

Breastfeeding: Treat it like a long journey rather than something you can just 'do' or be good at with no practice!

A Real Mama

Don't Forget to Take Care of You!

Finding Time for Yourself

Becoming a mom is the beginning of something so big and beautiful that will change you forever in the best ways possible. However, it is also the end (for a while, anyway) of the freedom in the life you knew before. It is normal and OK to mourn the leisure time and rest you might not have even realized you had before. Many new moms find that it's only once they have a tiny human attached to them 24/7 and have kissed their sleep schedule goodbye that they realize just how much rest and relaxation they actually had before.

Here's the thing, though: Taking care of a baby is a big commitment and a 'round-the-clock experience. You have got to carve out some time for self-care and breaks if you don't want to burnout, and to be the best version of yourself for that precious baby. This means filling up the occasional nap or post-bedtime break with something like a long bath followed by a face mask and Netflix rather than tidying up the house or folding baby clothes. It means taking the baby with you on fun errands you want to do, when possible. If you're itching to get out of the house, do so! You can take the "eat-sleep-change" show on the road with a little practice and some self-kindness.

Perhaps most importantly, you are going to have to learn to say "yes" when trusted people offer to help and to seek help when they don't. It can be hard to relinquish control when you're finding your footing as a new mom, but it's so important for you to have pockets of time, however brief, that are about nothing but you. This way, you will return to Baby refreshed and feeling like *you*, not just Mom.

Carving Out Time

Right now, your routine with Baby is very much centered around their needs, which is important. But think through the shape of your days and see where you can switch the focus to your own needs a bit. For example, a morning nap can happen in the stroller or baby carrier, so you can get fresh air. The evening bath can include a nice cup of your favorite tea. Better still, you can break up the monotony of Baby's care routine any time of day by inviting a close girlfriend over to catch up and enjoy an adult conversation.

Getting up and out for fresh air and light exercise is definitely a serotonin and endorphin boost if you're feeling healed enough for a walk and the weather is agreeable. But don't feel bad if you'd rather take care of yourself by baking a batch of your favorite cookies or binge-watching some good TV.

You'll find that you get the hang of taking care of your newborn pretty quickly, and while every day is a bit different, you will soon gain the confidence to figure out when and where you can fit some of your old favorite activities in while simultaneously taking care of the baby.

In a few months' time, they'll eat less often, nap more predictably, and be more portable. It might help to have something lined up now like a music or mom-and-me yoga class for when you and Baby feel ready; it might also feel best to not rush into any structured activity and just take life one day at a time. There are no right or wrong ways to take care of you. No one else is experiencing *your* postpartum journey, and this is a time when you need to be selfish—outside of the baby's needs, the only other concern you should have is with your own day-to-day happiness, rest, and fulfillment.

Taking Care of You

Many women find that incorporating some of their usual self-care routines into the start of the day with Baby helps them feel more like a whole person and not just a mom. If you enjoy doing your hair and makeup, hand Baby off to your partner or place them down safely in view, and make that time for yourself. If you have a clingy baby who doesn't like to be put down, you can try wearing them while you get ready.

Self-care can also be as simple as washing and moisturizing your face at the end of the day or making a brief phone call to someone who makes you laugh. And, as always, the journaling and mindfulness prompts at the end of every chapter in this book are there for you as you sort through your feelings and try to get in touch with your inner self.

Many moms enjoy getting up and dressed at the start of the day and closing out with their favorite nightly rituals, but self-care is different for everyone. Here is a list of activities that the moms we polled enjoyed in the first several weeks of their babies's lives:

- Walks around the corner and longer, more intense hikes once healed
- DIY manicure or pedicure or leaving the baby with a caregiver to go out and get a manicure at the nail salon
- Face / eye / hand / foot masks in the bathroom—especially while their partner gave the baby dinner or a bath!
- FaceTime or lunch with a good friend
- Aimless walks around a favorite store, cup of coffee in hand
- Reading a good book
- Sitting down to enjoy tea or coffee hot while the baby naps
- Flipping through magazines
- Scrapbooking or working on a baby book
- A long, hot shower

- "Absolute trash TV"
- Putting on makeup to feel like yourself
- Shopping online for new clothes that fit your postpartum body well
- Rewatching your old favorite movies (all comfort; no thought)
- Checking email (and it's OK if scanning through your work inbox makes you feel more like you, too!)

Safeguarding Your Down-Time

We cannot stress enough how important it is that you care for your mental health right now. There are some things you should consider doing right away to avoid needless anxiety at an already sensitive time:

1. Social media can be your fun friend or a major foe. Right now, put this book down and spend a solid twenty minutes unfollowing any group or individual that brings you stress, makes you worry about your baby or your parenting skills, causes any self-loathing or doubt, or has you stacking yourself up against other women based on looks, cleanliness of your home, etc. ....OK, now that you're back and that's done: During this tender time, use social media as you wish to share photos, videos, highlights, or updates about your

little one with friends and family. You may even like to incorporate some mindless scrolling into your list of me-time activities. But the moment any person or entity in your feed starts to upset or stress you, it's time to get them out of your path.

2. Avoid people or places that stress you out. It should go without saying, but many of us have pushy aunts or sisters-in-law, seemingly important errands that make us feel anxious, etc. You will have all the time in the world to handle these people and situations when the postpartum period has waned; right now you have to put a little protective barrier wall around yourself and say "no" to people, places, or obligations that drain you mentally and emotionally.

3. "Healthy" comes in different shapes, styles, and sizes. Some moms experience an easy birth, get lucky with a good sleeper, and heal quickly. Good for them! If it's not on your radar to get back into a workout routine, *please* listen to your body and don't. Right now, the two things that matter most for your health are hydration and rest. Do not try any sort of "diet" or force yourself back into the gym, especially in the name of self-care.

What might be the healthiest thing in the world for you right now is a heaping plate of your favorite foods and a nice long nap. The world is not waiting anxiously for you to lose weight and return to your pre-baby body and nor should you be. Trying to whip yourself radically back into shape is *not* "me-time" or self-care; with your doctor's "OK," light exercise might feel good. If not, avoid it.

When the Baby Sleeps...

People love the old adage, "Sleep when the baby sleeps!" Meanwhile, most new moms want to pull their hair out when they're told this. I remember feeling so pressured by the advice to take a nap when my first baby was doing so. It might have sounded ridiculous to my friends and family, but as exhausted as I was, sleeping did not come naturally when any of my newborns napped, unless they were in someone else's care.

Here's the thing: When you're a new mom, you find yourself responsible for someone else's life, nourishment, comfort, and care at all times. *Yes*, it's exhausting, but for plenty of newborn mamas, the anxiety and worry or just plain feeling like you want some time for yourself make it hard to nap when the baby naps. If you're able to lie down and rest when they do, that's wonderful. If not, don't pressure yourself to nap just because someone else says you should.

There are ways to rest that have nothing to do with napping. You can try meditating in a dim room, putting on some mindless TV while lying on the couch, or doing some gentle yoga with YouTube. You can also refer to our bullets above for activities that will fill Baby's nap time without exerting effort on housework, bill paying, or other "catch-up" deliverables that bring you stress.

But remember, this time is all about you. If light housework or organizing Baby's closet is cathartic and sets you up for a more relaxing evening or weekend ahead, do that. Sometimes it's hard to decide for ourselves what the "best" way to spend any amount of time is as new moms. It seems the Internet and well-meaning friends, family, and even strangers all have plenty of ideas and opinions. The bottom line is that this is *your* postpartum period, and all that matters is what makes you feel good.

It's important to note that some babies really sleep best on their parents. This can feel relentless and limiting, especially if you're trying to "soak it all up" and "be in the moment." Mama, you're only human, and it's normal to feel touched out and overwhelmed when the baby has been in your arms or on your chest all day. Get cozy and give yourself permission to do absolutely nothing today but hold that sweet babe and force yourself to relax. You can still take a break without waking them by doing at least half the things on our bullet list above, from snacking to watching trash TV and catching up with friends over the phone.

A Little Help Goes a Long Way

Speaking of friends... They say it takes a village to raise a child, and the truth is, our modern society, built around an emphasis on the nuclear family, means that many of us are without that village. And to be fair, it's also possible that Great Aunt Mildred or your pushy neighbor might mean well in offering to "help" with Baby, but something in your gut just says "no" to leaving your precious little one in certain people's care.

You call the shots. Full stop. It's a really good idea to let your partner share the workload of caring for Baby (and letting them take care of you, too!), but as far as other people's offers of help go, you have a right to be discerning. That said, if you do not have any nearby family members who want to help and are capable of doing so, do yourself the favor of hiring someone you can trust, even just for a few hours a week.

Breaks are needed for your sanity, and as long as your baby is well taken care of, you should use this time to do things for yourself that make you feel more like you.

Take a Mindful Minute

Journal Prompts:

- *Snaps for Mama.* Be a little self-congratulating today. You deserve it. List anything you did for yourself today and be proud. It could be as simple as making a fresh cup of coffee and ignoring the laundry.

While your baby is growing every day, you are also growing into the role of motherhood. Be proud of the work you've done this week or day for the baby, and also of all you've done to make time for yourself.

- *Mommy's Bucket List.* These types of lists serve as a way to daydream and make fun plans for yourself, but better yet, they pull you to make them all a reality. Write down all of the "just for me" things you hope to accomplish in the next few months and come back to this entry to check them off as you go. (**Pro Tip:** It feels *really* good to check things off, so you might want to put a couple things on there that you've already done!)

Mindfulness Exercise:

This one is for tomorrow morning. You are going to start the day with your own self-interest as part of the equation. You are going to wake up and do one thing for yourself as soon as you have fed or tended to your baby for the first time in the day. You are going to brush your teeth and hair, eat breakfast, and remember yourself throughout the day. Tonight, before you fall asleep, picture tomorrow. Picture yourself like you would a friend—someone who needs and deserves love and someone who will get it.

Being a mother is the best reason to
take good care of yourself.

YOU ARE NOT ALONE

Navigating Relationships & Isolation

In the early weeks and months with Baby, you might feel alienated and isolated as a natural consequence of this new lifestyle. In time, you'll be back in the world on a more normal schedule, with and without your baby in tow, but for now, all of this staying at home and doing the same things over and over can be hard.

Additionally, many new moms feel their personal relationships start to strain under the heaviness of the new role of motherhood and how little time it leaves for others. The takeaway from this chapter will be that you are not alone in these feelings. Open communication and seeking connection will help, as will focusing on those people who truly want to be there for you. Some of them, you may not even know yet!

Keeping Your Partner Close

You're both tired and overwhelmed as you wade through this "new normal" while focusing on your baby's health and contentment.

Sometimes we can feel lonely and miss our partner even when we're right next to each other; what you're missing is the closeness and previous way of relating.

This will pass, but in the meantime, there are ways to make it better. Your partner is not a mind-reader, and you should tell them what you want and need, which will help you feel more supported and secure. Something as simple as closing out the day by watching an episode of a TV show you both enjoy or having a nice dinner at home with no phones or other distractions, can help you reconnect and strengthen your bond despite all the changes in the home. When you feel ready and have a trustworthy sitter you can use, date nights will bridge your old relationship to your new one. This adults-only time away allows us to connect deeply and share what's on our minds while just having some much-needed fun (and eating dinner while it's hot, which now feels like a luxury).

In the meantime—this might sound crazy!—but when you have a tiny baby, it is actually a great time to take them with you on a date. The baby will sleep most of the time, and you'll have the chance to get out of the house together and feel a bit like your old selves. Bring some bottles or wear a nursing-friendly outfit and get out! My husband and I discovered this hack early in our eldest's newborn phase and soon made a habit of getting dressed up and going to super-fancy restaurants with her in one of our arms. We figured, "Now is the time!" before she turned into a toddler who was likelier to make noise and a scene in a nice restaurant. Brunch is also a fun way to get out of the house with or without your baby and just chat.

If there is limited time or budget for dates, something as simple as taking a long drive together while the baby sleeps in the backseat can be really good for your relationship. Open up to each other, making sure that you share your feelings about all of this change but also listen to theirs. Even if you are the primary caregiver for the baby, your partner's life has changed, too.

Giving them the space to communicate their feelings with you will help keep you both connected, rather than withdrawing and letting resentment build up. Your relationship as you knew it is not over, it has just changed and had a new layer added. You two will grow closer than ever before, but you have to do the work to let that new closeness bloom.

Friendships as a New Mom

In addition to your relationship with your partner, you might feel your friendships changing right now. If you're lucky, there are women in your life who "get it" and want to stick around. Most new moms, though, have some friends who either don't have kids or have older kids, and just don't stay as connected or show enough interest.

Trying to maintain any good friendship is admirable, but your focus right now needs to be on yourself and your little family. Some friendships will have a quiet period and grow back to normal later;

some may never be the same. And still others are just waiting to be found, formed, and nurtured.

Learning to Let Go

It can be hard to say goodbye to longtime friendships, but you know in your heart when someone who's been there in the past is acting distant, cold, disinterested in your new life as a mom, or otherwise hurting you. If you've tried and aren't getting anything in return, just know it's OK to walk away for a while. There are many reasons why someone without kids or with older kids may be distant right now, but it's not your job to seek out those reasons and beg people to be in your life.

If a friend is quietly struggling with infertility, unhappy in her family or relationship, or just doesn't enjoy being around kids and babies, she might pull away. Maybe you and these individual friends will mend things later, but for now, you have to remember that protective wall around yourself and your family that we touched on in Chapter Three and phase out people whose actions make you feel hurt and isolated.

Keeping Your Closest Circle

Those who do show up are gold. Even more so if they drop meals off or let you know they're there without pushing past your boundaries. But remember: Everyone's postpartum journey is different, so even your friends with children may not know exactly what you need right now. *Let them know.* Be honest about not feeling comfortable going out in public right now, or not wanting anyone else to hold the baby, or conversely, needing someone to come over and hold them while you take a shower.

Let your friends who have shown up know how they can best support you right now, because that is what they want to do. Don't feel guilty for not being able to reciprocate right now; a "thank you" and a hug are all a true friend needs.

Text & Go Friendships

Long-distance, working, or other friends who don't have the physical time or ease of getting to you right now can still be a huge support system. Again, they may not know exactly what you need, so tell them. When I had my first baby, I was living in a new city with no friends who had babies, and I felt totally alone. I found that reigniting some old college and high school friendships over text was an incredible support.

These fellow moms who lived a plane ride away but had known me on-and-off since we were kids ourselves were such an amazing source of kindness, comfort, and information as I navigated my changing body, the baby's needs, and all sorts of questions and worries in the early days. It was such a beautiful thing when I was able to be that "text support" person to my long-distance best friend the following year when she gave birth to her first.

Text-and-go friends don't need to live far away; life is just busy for moms and it's normal if you don't have a lot of time to be together in person. Texting a friend while you have a baby sleeping in your arms is a great reminder that you are not alone and that there are people in your world who love and support you, even when you don't have the time or energy for a lunch date or even a long phone call.

Popping Out When You Can

To that end, getting out with or without your baby can seem daunting in the beginning. Start small with a stroller walk or a quick drive to a nearby cafe for just coffee. Don't be embarrassed if you're toting an enormous diaper bag packed to the brim with clothes and supplies; whatever you have to do to feel prepared and confident leaving the house is fine. Plan to stay for 20 minutes and check in with yourself after that time has passed. If you want to stay longer, do.

Maybe in a few weeks you'll feel up to lunch or something more; maybe not. Ease back into getting out of the house and be kind to yourself while you get your footing as a new mom, especially on-the-go. And never feel guilty about saying "no" to an invitation or plan that doesn't sound enjoyable, relaxing, or manageable right now. You'll have plenty of time and opportunity for socializing in the months and years to come; right now you're in your newborn bubble, and it's up to you to decide what people and activities are welcome in the bubble.

Merging Your Worlds

Another great way to keep close to your friends is to invite them into your mommy-life. "Errand friends" are some of my favorite ones to have. A friend who will come with you to do the shopping or pick out a new stroller. Who will take your morning walk with you just to catch up with no meal or spending involved, or just sit by your side while you fold laundry.

You can also have a friend over for a quiet lunch or afternoon of binge-watching TV together. It doesn't have to be fancy, and it doesn't matter what your home looks like. A true friend wants to be there because they want to be with you. That said, if you're missing your old life of dinner and drinks on the town, you can also bring a taste of it into your new life. Invite a good friend over, order or cook something delicious, open a good bottle of wine, and enjoy a lovely evening without ever having to leave the house.

Building Mommy Connections

In addition to finding new ways to strengthen old bonds, this is an exciting time to explore the possibility of meeting friends who are in your same season of life. This is not to discount existing friends, but some of the best friends you'll grow with in the next several years are the ones who had new babies right around when you did.

Seek out baby groups via your local mom connections on Facebook, community centers or places of worship, and word of mouth. You can also ask at the pediatrician's or your doctor's office if they have any advice on where you can connect with other new moms. And even though your baby is too young for the playground, a stroll in a local park is a great first step toward meeting other new moms out and about.

Don't be afraid to say hi. It might feel awkward, but if you see another mother with a young baby in a coffee shop, in line at the supermarket, etc., she might really need that "hello" more than you know. I was sitting on a lounge chair by a public pool once when I struck up a conversation with another mom who was there with her young baby. She ended up inviting me over for coffee, and nine years and three long-distance moves later, I am going to visit her in another country this year to catch up. That is how close and important a bond can stem from a quick hi in the newborn (or any!) shared season of motherhood.

Other new moms are in the trenches with you. They want connection, too. Not everyone is going to be your new best friend, but you never know who might be ready to step into your life and stick until you try.

Take a Mindful Minute

Journal Prompts:

- Relationship Affirmation: *Our love created this baby and has turned us into a family. Nurturing that love is as important as nurturing the baby and family.*

  Spend some time writing down moments of connection where you felt at home in your relationship recently and some of your old favorite things to do together. In the weeks to come, see how some of those old traditions can work themselves back into your new life as parents.

- Friendship Affirmation: *I am worthy of true friendship and love, and the people who want to be in my life are the ones who deserve my time.*

  Do a little mental scan of friends who you can count on (near or far), and consider this entry a mini-contacts list for moments when you need someone to talk to.

Mindfulness Exercise:

Setting intentions is a fundamental part of any mindfulness journey. These do not need to be extremely detailed or heartfelt; sometimes an intention is just a word. Close your eyes and take a moment to set an intention or two about connection. This can be aimed at your own sense of loneliness and not tied to any particular relationship, or it could be very much tied to your partner or friend(s). Set this intention now and make a habit of returning to it whenever you struggle in the coming weeks and months.

Maybe your intention with your partner is "patience" or even "more cuddling." When they frustrate you, you'll return to this intention and how it can help. Maybe your intention is tied to a specific friend you want to make an effort to call more often, and when you start to feel panicked or lonely, you'll remember that calling them is always an option. Maybe it's an all-encompassing intention like "openness" or to simply forgive yourself for not having a lot of time right now for socializing.

This is your moment to reflect on how you can feel better in your relationships, and always go back to those affirmations above whenever you need them. Yes, you are important to your baby, but there are other people who love you, and now is their time to support you by showing that love.

A sleeping baby is the new
'Happy Hour'!

The Perfect Mom Doesn't Exist

Expectations vs. Reality

Alright, Mama, it's time to get real.

We spend nine months, if not more, planning out what kind of cute and "together" moms we are going to be, only to discover that Week Two rolls around and we still feel like we've been hit by a bus and spend the whole day feeding and changing our babies.

There's a secret about motherhood that really shouldn't be one, but in this age of Instagram and Pinterest, where motherhood has been bottled, shined up, and commodified, it's important that you listen in:

There are no perfect mothers.

It's OK if your house gets messy. Getting back into your jeans six weeks after delivery sounds glorious, but it didn't happen to me or a single woman I know. You will mess up. You will lose patience. Your house will sometimes get disastrous. These are all part of the secret, but the bottom line is this: Motherhood is going to be wonderful, beautiful, fulfilling, and life-changing, but it is not going to look exactly how you imagined it.

Slash Your Grand Plans

It's lovely to picture your maternity leave taking place in coffee shops or starting a new time-consuming hobby you've always dreamed about. Wearing matching mommy-and-me outfits and taking circuit workout classes with your little one nestled nearby. It's even possible that some of that might happen in time.

But honestly, the sheer work of the first several months of a new baby's life leaves most moms feeling tired, worn out, and not up for much. Allow yourself to slash, or at least shelve, all the grandiose ideas of how you'd spend this time and just focus on caring for yourself and your baby as best you can from one day to the next.

Leaning In to What Works

In addition to how we thought we'd act, who among us didn't have a picture of how things would look? I pictured a serene home with a few corners peppered by sweet monochrome wooden toys and a fancy play mat for tummy time. I even asked the sales associate who helped my husband and me while we registered for our first baby if she could show me some "chic-looking swings and bouncers." The way she tried to hold back her laughter was admirable; three months and an actual baby later, my living room was a sea of rainbow-hued apparatus that bobbed, glowed, and sang to a degree that was just this side of vulgar.

Guess what? My baby loved it all.

You have every right to plan out and design your home in a way that feels good for your senses and makes you happy. But please give yourself permission to cave in on the gear and toys that will make your life easier and happier as a mom, and know that most of those bloggers with pristine living rooms have a pile of plastic stuff hidden just outside the frame.

Social Media is a Lie

Speaking of bloggers, it's more important now than ever before in your life as a woman to remind yourself, often and wholeheartedly, that the images we see online are not authentic. This goes beyond airbrushing and filters, which are problematic enough.

"Mom Content" has taken on a life of its own, and daily we are hit with photo after reel after fabricated story. You've seen them all—perfect Sunday afternoons frolicking in the yard in all white clothing; sourdough starters giving life to a new mother-daughter hobby; postpartum moms in fitted clothing wearing babies on their chests while they deep-clean their homes or head out for a fancy lunch and shopping.

It can be really hard to resist the pressure to stack ourselves up against these other mothers serving fictionalized versions of motherhood to the world. Try to remember that there is no such thing as "having it all," and if you are feeling like only so much can happen in a day, you are very much in the majority. This is especially true when you have a new baby and get very few breaks to do things for yourself.

The Unseen Damage of Pinterest Parenting

As you grow as a mom alongside your blossoming baby, remember that this obsession with DIY-ing the details of a gorgeous nursery, creating sensory play stations for your little one, and throwing the best birthday parties is also pressure and noise you just don't need.

Pinterest and blogs are great for advice and ideas when you are looking for something specific, but if you can't trust yourself not to go down a rabbit hole that's going to leave you feeling like you haven't accomplished much lately, don't do it. Caring for a new baby is accomplishment enough.

Beauty in the Everyday

This is a time in your life when you are collecting warm and precious memories for later. Right now, you might feel irritated by a messy countertop or a few piles of errant laundry, but later, all you'll want is to look back and know that you took the time to rest and enjoy your baby as they grow. Take all the pictures and videos you can, and make sure you're in many of them.

Strive to find the best in your days, even when that's hard. Or rather, especially when things are a bit hard. One mom we spoke to shared this hilarious tidbit about the listless period as a new mom:

One time I had a handful of baby sick and didn't know what to do with it, so I just wiped it in my hair!

One morning I was making myself a cup of coffee and accidentally poured in half a bag of defrosted breast milk instead of reaching for the milk carton. These ridiculous stories where we're caught at our rawest and most sleep-deprived will be touching anecdotes of this unique time later.

Among the handfuls of baby sick and breast milk-laden coffee, find joy in the simplest moments and ignore the pressure to match, organize, laminate, decorate, or "have it all." The fact is, you have your baby and a safe home to raise them in; that right there means you already have it all.

Focusing on the Small & Important

The way their eyelids flutter open and their tiny fingers wrap around yours. The sweet smell of their breath and how soft their hair is to the touch. The "newborn scrunch" when you pick them up and they pull their little legs up and in. These are the aesthetics that outweigh the perfect paint color or a well-stocked and organized pantry.

Relish in the tiny things, because later on, they will feel like the biggest. You might not have decorated a Pinterest-worthy nursery or be learning a new language right now, but things are beautiful just like this. In your life, becoming a parent will be one of, if not *the* most profound examples of the difference between expectations and reality. Embrace it, because with the right mindset, you might just find the reality is so much better than you expected.

Take a Mindful Minute

Journal Prompt:

- Turning messes into magic... Look around the room. Write down the things that visually are the most different from your expectations or hopes of motherhood. It could be as simple as your outfit or the fact that you haven't left the house today. Now revisit each of them and write beside them what the positives are.

Examples: A full diaper pail. (My baby is digesting and thriving.)

An ugly plastic swing. (I have somewhere safe to put the baby down and get a hands-free moment.)

Mindfulness Exercise:

Embracing and remembering key feelings can make it easier to get through hard moments as they come up. Look back on something that happened today or yesterday that was totally counter to what you envisioned your "new mom life" to be like. This can also be applied to not a moment or emotion but a physical thing like that dreaded laundry pile. Now picture that frustrating hurdle laid out as if it were a map. There are many facets to it; search among the rubble of crumbled expectations for the pops of new information and bright spots you didn't expect on this landscape.

Like the journaling exercise, as you lay out the visuals of your challenges in this unspoken and unnecessary attempt at perfection, little surprises will pop up. Yes, you have more laundry than ever before, but simply moving those baskets out of the living room and thus out of sight for a few days will help. And when you do so, catching sight of those tiny and sweet outfits will be a gentle reminder that this new territory is not as daunting as it is beautiful.

No-one gets the hat trick! Kind pregnancy, dream birth, easy breastfeeding journey...

And if they tell you they did...they're lying!

A Real Mama

Bad Feelings Are Normal

Anxiety, Negative Thoughts & Trauma

We've discussed expectation vs. reality in terms of how things are and how they look, but we have not dived too deeply into the realm of how you expected to *feel*. Before Baby's arrival, many of us picture the newborn period as being a blissful and relaxing time where we'll soak up the cuddles and feel a bit more like ourselves after pregnancy.

It's great if you do feel that way some or most days, but for many new moms, the bliss is often threatened by intrusive thoughts, new worries and fears, or anxiety or sadness that coincide with recovery from the trauma of pregnancy and birth.

Especially if you've never experienced acute anxiety before, this can be startling. Just know that you are not alone in these hard feelings and that you deserve to take the steps needed to feel better.

Anxiety & Fears

You become a mom, and suddenly you're responsible for the safety and care of this precious, vulnerable little being who is entirely dependent on you. Worrying about them—almost to the point of excess—is definitely in the realm of normal. Especially in this day and age where we have the whole world at our fingertips and hear or read so many tales of caution and hardship constantly, it can be difficult to focus on the positive and push negative thoughts away.

After giving birth to my second daughter, I was in a constant state of worry that something terrible would happen to me or my husband and that our girls would be left without us. These thoughts rendered me afraid of driving or even leaving the house much on foot, and when it came to the baby, those worries were even worse.

Her safety was a constant cause for concern that made it hard for me to enjoy the day-to-day. I had met so many new moms since having my first and was more tapped into the mommy community; it's like knowing more made me even more terrified that something awful could happen to my baby. I was possessive of her and didn't want family members holding her or passing her around. I had trouble sleeping because watching her breathe made me feel like I could somehow control her well-being. It was definitely a difficult period, but with therapy and the passage of time, things got better.

Self-Doubt & Negative Self-Talk

Another area where many moms struggle is worrying that they are not enough. Not good enough, not organized enough, not energized enough... There are so many extensions of this type of thinking. Lots of new parents speak unkindly to themselves and take the blame for things outside their control.

One great way to combat these feelings is to build a thicker and stronger cocoon around yourself and your family. If the women in your baby group are comparing and bragging about their baby's achievements or their own, it might not be the best group for you. If a blog or Instagram account you turn to for parenting advice starts to make you feel like you're missing the mark, now would be a great time to unfollow.

So much of parenting is trial-and-error, learning as we go, and will be different for each baby and family. Don't let other people's schedules, homes, feeding styles, or other factors make you feel like less of an awesome mom. When the negative thoughts try to intrude, head to the mindfulness exercises at the end of this chapter to help your mind and body get past them.

Mommy Guilt

Let me tell it to you straight: There is not a mother alive who does not or has not ever experienced some kind of mom-guilt. It's just part of the gig unfortunately, and it'll get better in time. But even as you and your baby grow, there will be new junctions that stir up fresh crops of guilt, and you'll be combating them throughout the years. Now is a great time to practice pushing these feelings aside and moving past them.

You might feel guilty for carving out time for yourself or leaving the baby with your partner or a family member to get a break. Please try to force yourself through this feeling and enjoy your time away. Even if it's just an hour here or there, our mental health relies on breaks and rest, and you deserve this. No one can do it all, all the time, without growing resentful and just plain exhausted.

It took some time to get used to, but looking back, I'm so glad I pushed myself through the guilt to get little breaks when my children were brand new. Now that I have two elementary-aged kids and a toddler, the pattern has been set, so I feel no guilt at all leaving them with their dad or a sitter to take care of my own needs sometimes. Reuniting a few hours later is always the best feeling for everyone involved.

As you grow into your role as a mother, you'll find that guilt creeping in. Just remember that it is natural and something we all experience. Stay-at-home moms often report feeling guilty that they don't contribute to the finances of the home or that they are liable to be less patient after a long day at home with the children than, say, a spouse who hasn't seen the kids all day. Working mothers often feel guilty that they are not physically present when they're at work; missing our kids makes many of us feel guilty, whether we're gone for an hour or 9.

The thing is, all your child cares about is that you love and appreciate them. That you care for them in your way, and by the way, a big part of that is finding loving caregivers to step in when you can't be there. No matter what is making you feel guilty as a mom now or in the future, always return to the bottom line, which is that no one is perfect and all that matters to your baby is that you love them and do your best.

Birth & Other Trauma

Pregnancy alone is a trauma. Your body has stretched and grown; you've been fatigued and overwhelmed, and you've suffered from all manner of strange new symptoms you've never experienced before. Many moms also go on to experience birth trauma, which can be really hard to get past, especially in those first few months.

Maybe your birth had a degree of emergency, turned into a cesarean, or ended with a NICU stay for Baby. Other types of birth trauma include minor to major injuries, giving birth after a loss, or simply not having the support in the room that you would have wanted. For many moms, not having the birth they expected can feel like a trauma, too, even if nothing actually went "wrong."

All of these feelings are valid, normal, and will pass. Ignoring them doesn't help, but talking to your partner, parents, a trusted friend, or a professional really can. My first birth ended in an emergency c-section after I had famously told my husband to ignore all of the c-section information at our birthing classes because "I just wasn't going to have one." There is so much that can end up out of our control during delivery, and it's hard to grapple with those feelings later.

How to Cope

Bonding with your baby and focusing on the day-to-day tasks in front of you can be quite healing. Staying as rested and hydrated as possible helps, too. Sometimes, when I struggled as a brand-new mommy, I found that the fundamentals of caring for myself and the baby made things so much better. It's really hard to work through difficult emotions on an empty stomach or when you're weary and dehydrated.

Talking openly to your partner about these feelings is also really helpful. Very often, they will have no idea the complexity of your emotions, and it feels good to let them out. There might be parts of your anxiety-fueled thinking that can be assuaged with their help (like my husband offering to take shifts watching our daughter sleep so that I could rest). Sometimes it's as simple as a big hug and being reminded that you are doing a great job and do not need to feel guilty about a thing.

Friends who've been there can also be a limitless source of comfort and advice. Don't be afraid to share how you're feeling with your girlfriends, even if it's only to say honestly, "I'm feeling too anxious to be out in a crowd today; can we catch up at my house or over the phone instead?" Share your feelings with the people who love you. It only serves to help in your healing.

It's OK to Get Help

Any new mom who worries excessively about their health and safety or their little ones', is suffering from severe guilt, or has unresolved pregnancy and birth trauma needs to know that there is absolutely no shame in seeking professional help. Mental health care is one of the best tools for creating the life you want.

Whether you choose talk therapy, speak to your doctor about medication options, or work with an app that features tools to help you, there are many avenues to explore on your healing journey. Time is a great healer, but it's OK to look into ways to feel better now. Your baby loves you just the way you are. Love yourself enough to take care of that sweet baby's mother in any way you can.

Regaining Confidence

Hitting our stride as mothers can come on all at once or in drips. Some days we look around and think, "I've really got this parenting thing down." Others feel like we're living outside of our bodies, looking down on a listless and overwhelmed woman who isn't cut out for the job.

As we discussed in Chapter One, observe and notice the negative feelings, but don't feed them and head into a spiral with them. Remind yourself at every turn that you are new at this, that you are learning as you go, and that you and your baby are doing great.

Little by little, you will overcome anxiety, self-doubt, negative feelings, and trauma. On the other side of this tough adjustment period is a mom who feels confident, happy, and secure. She will always leave a little room for learning and growth, because that's what mothers do. She will always feel a little pang when she is apart from her babies, because that is what love does. But she is going to be OK. You will make sure of it.

Take a Mindful Minute

Journal Prompt:

- *Worry Journal:* This is a practice used by many therapists and anxiety experts to help people work through negative or intrusive thoughts. It sounds counterintuitive to lean into your fears by listing them, but many people find that writing down everything they are worried about can actually help.

Naming the fears one by one, as a list of single words or in detailed sentences, start your worry journal today. You can make this a separate journal from your other one or set them up in a new section. This practice allows you to get the fears out without heading down a path with them. Once you're done and see them on the page, it's time to let go of them for the day and just enjoy your baby.

- *Anxiety & Trauma Affirmations:* Hold onto whichever one(s) you need. Say them in the mirror or write them in your journal, and elaborate on them below.

My birth experience does not define my motherhood. My baby is here and safe, and I am letting go of guilt or sadness over their delivery.This is just my anxiety talking. My baby is well taken care of, and I am doing everything I can to keep our family safe.

I don't need to feel guilty for leaving my baby in trusted hands. A happy and rested mom is important.

There are no perfect mothers. What I am is the best mother for my baby.

Mindfulness Exercise:

Aside from ruminating on the affirmations above, this is a good point in your new-mommy trajectory to work on replacing negative thoughts with positive ones. It doesn't happen immediately, but make a practice of this meditation, and it can only help your healing journey.

Bring to mind one of the intrusive thoughts you've been having. Add visuals by either closing your eyes and focusing on the images that come to mind or staring at a blank wall to allow your mind to conjure them. Whether you're focused on a specific fear, mom-guilt, or pregnancy or birth-related trauma, look closely at the image that comes to mind. Remember what was said or conjure the sounds you associate with the painful thought. Now imagine silencing the whole situation and adding a new script. Picture an "override" of the hard feeling.

If it's tied to something that actually happened, rewrite history a bit and add a happier ending. Imagine a supportive loved one in the room, guiding you through the birth you didn't want. Think of the last time you felt guilty, and imagine someone you trust stepping in and telling you what a good job you're doing. When it comes to fears and worries, replace the image of the worst with a calm and happy outcome. This is not easy and takes practice, but the more mindfulness time you put into it, the more naturally it will come. The goal here is to eventually replace those negative thoughts right away, without even needing to take a moment to meditate.

For now, all you need to do is close your eyes and try.

Remember: it's okay to ask for help.
It's okay not to be okay.

You Do You, Boo

Boundaries & Unsolicited Advice

You're new to this whole parenting thing, but that does not mean you don't know what you're doing. Don't be afraid to ask questions of your friends, doctor, parents, and anyone else who can give you the advice you seek. But also remember that this is your baby, and you don't need to listen to, let alone heed, all of the advice thrown at you.

In pregnancy, you probably experienced the "warnings" about how you'd never sleep again, along with a heavy dose of naysayers trying to come between you and a morning cup of coffee or a plate of runny eggs (whatever *they* were told not to consume during pregnancy and is now considered safe). This doesn't stop once the baby is here; the advice will get worse before it gets better. Now is the time to toughen up your exterior and set some boundaries. From unwanted visits to things you just don't need to hear, people will try to barge in; you need to set yourself up with some tools to prevent them from affecting you.

Make a Visitor Plan

Before Baby's arrival, or as soon as you're home and settled, talk to your partner about expectations and comfort level with guests. Many people will want to come by and see the baby, but even though they are coming from a good place, it's OK to say "no" or "not now" any time that you want to.

First, you should feel completely unburdened by other people coming in when you are sleep-deprived and finding your footing as a new mom. It adds pressure to tidy up, shower, and hand your baby over to a visitor, none of which may be on the cards on any given day. Decide how long you want visits to last, what times of day you are happy to have people stop by, and which days of the week work best. Expect these to change, and maybe lessen, as you go.

Be upfront with anyone who asks to stop by, and don't ever feel bad about declining. People who are offering to visit for the right reasons will respect and understand your boundaries. The feelings of anyone who is visiting to serve their own interests are not your business or problem. This is *your* baby and *your* postpartum experience; what you want and what you say are all that matter.

When Family Pushes Too Hard

Even the people you love the most can come on too strong when you're adjusting to life with a new baby. I had family members show up unannounced or with little notice, sometimes even sitting down on my couch and asking me to make them food! The audacity made my husband and I jump to put together an email to all family members with our parameters about time, days, and length of visits henceforth, as suggested above. This helped a lot, especially because we never directed it at one single person, so nobody got defensive or felt pushed away.

It isn't just unexpected or too-long visits that can be tough, though. Holidays and extended family dinners, if they pop up during your postpartum period, can bring stress and drama. From people wanting to take the baby from you and hold them for ages or pass them around to Aunt Susie giving you all her obnoxious and outdated parenting advice from the 80's, a family gathering can go from awesome to awful quick.

Surviving—and even enjoying—these gatherings is possible when you put yourself and your family first. A great way to prevent people from picking up and passing around the baby too much is to wear them in a sling or carrier. This necessitates your granting them permission first, since Baby is attached to you! Also, work on speaking up when Baby is in someone else's arms and starts to cry or needs to be fed or changed; you are Mom, and it's more important to take care of your little one's needs than to let a relative hold on longer than they should.

Having canned responses ready for any unwanted advice is also helpful. You're bound to get lots of it around family in particular because sometimes when people feel close to us, social norms slip and they'll say things they wouldn't to a stranger. Whether it's about feeding style, how Baby is dressed, what you should be doing for sleep, etc., unless you ask for and appreciate the advice, there is no need to engage and turn it into a conversation. Here are some phrases you can try or alter to feel more like you:

"Thank you, but I'm not looking for advice on that right now."

"Thanks for sharing that with me! Can you please pass the salt?" (A direct subject change drives home the point that you are not going to get into this with them.)

"That's an interesting take, but we're happy with our choice."

"They're all so different! I'm glad you found what worked for you, and we are doing the same."

These are just some examples of phrases you can use when faced with unwanted advice. In time, you'll become more confident in shutting critics down (even loving ones!), but until then, having a scripted response ready is helpful.

Overcoming Negativity

It's not just family that can overstep; I remember being absolutely flabbergasted the first time a stranger walked up to me in public and criticized me. In my case, it was for the large bow I had put on my daughter that day—something I never would have imagined anyone would care about or comment on. I was so flustered that I felt tears stinging in my eyes right away and couldn't come up with a reply, so I just walked away slowly. I wish I could go back and give that new mom I was at the time a big hug and tell her I was doing a good job and that the baby's hair bow was of nobody else's concern.

Aside from these random critiques, you'll probably hear lots of warnings about the future. "Take her out now before she's a toddler and you can't go anywhere." Or my personal favorite, when you're struggling with a crying baby in public, "Just wait! It gets so much worse." *What?!*

Why would anyone say things like this? You are probably wondering. I've put a lot of thought into, and done much research on this topic, and it pretty much comes down to their own miserable regrets or circumstances. The human experience is all about connecting and relating; we see another mother out in the world, and we want to find a string between us. Something that denotes our shared experience. But when someone is not happy in their life or is currently facing regrets about how they handled things earlier, sometimes the only mode of relating they can find is to try and "warn" you about what's to come. Remember, this is *their* experience; their negativity has nothing to do with *your* life or future.

When you're struggling with a crying baby in public and someone chimes in to say that life will be much worse when they're older and to "enjoy them now," it can feel depressing, stressful, and hopeless. Like you have nothing to look forward to with your baby and that you should feel guilty about the fact that you're having a hard moment. We'll dive deeper with a meditation on this at the end of the chapter, but the key takeaway here is to not let these "warnings" affect you.

Remind yourself that this person is having a hard time and unfairly (and perhaps unknowingly) taking it out on you.

I used to worry that I wouldn't enjoy my children as they got older; so many people constantly told me that the newborn stage was the easiest and it was all downhill from there. To be honest, the newborn stage can be really hard, so that was worrying and sad to hear. I can tell you with confidence that these people are wrong. With my children spread from young toddler to late elementary, each stage has its challenges and absolute triumphs. Watching them grow and become their own little people is beautiful beyond my dreams. Ignore anyone who tells you differently.

Confidence is Key

Sometimes the old adage about faking it 'til you make it applies to parenting. It can definitely be true when it comes to feeling confident about your choices for your children and combating negative comments about parenting and kids in general.

The scenarios outlined above are good places for a scripted response to fire back when met with unwarranted advice or "warnings." Try some of these and see which feels most natural for you, or use them as a guide to come up with something in your own words.

In response to a comment about how your baby is dressed:

"Thanks for noticing his sweet outfit! I love dressing him. Have a great day!"

When met with commentary about feeding, outerwear, sleep, schedules, etc.:

"I'm actually not looking for feedback on that right now."

"All set on that topic. Thanks!"

"I know you mean well, but I don't need any tips in that area."

When confronted with warnings about the future or told to 'enjoy them now, while you still can!':

"I'm just so happy to have her; I'm not really thinking about that right now."

"I'm sure I'll figure that out when I get there."

"I enjoy being a mom so much now, and I'm sure I'll love it then, too."

"This moment is the one I'm focused on, but thanks!"

In time, you will reach a point where sharing sentiments like these becomes a reflex because you have grown in your confidence as a mother. Right now, use them as a shield against unwanted and undeserved negativity.

Every Baby is Different

Of course, the most blatant thing to notice here is that not everything works for every family and every baby. Just like the concepts focused on in our chapter on feeding styles, many parenting decisions will be tailored to your values, lifestyle, upbringing, means, and desires and will even vary from one child to the next.

All I could do was throw my hands up and laugh when I realized, three weeks into having my second baby, that bedtime with her was going to be completely different than it was with her big sister. I had to change my entire approach to scheduling, swaddling, and how to put her down at night and for naps after thinking I really had a good system ready from my first.

Babies are people, too, and parenting doesn't come with a user's manual. If you are seeking advice from people you trust, remember that you don't have to heed it all. If you are just out in the world trying to live and parent, and people barge in with unwarranted commentary, you have every right to shut it down and keep going about your day.

Take a Mindful Minute

Journal Prompt:

- *Now & Later* – Sometimes it's easy to get lost in the monotony of the day-to-day care of a newborn. If you've received "warnings" lately about how much you'll miss this time and you're feeling stressed about that, a great exercise is to write down some of your favorite things about right now and some things you're looking forward to doing with your baby when they're older.

- *Confidence in Parenting* – Those people who try to "help" but are actually dragging you down have no place in your journal or your headspace. Take some time today to write about your recent wins and little ways you've succeeded as a parent, whether that's a big milestone achieved or a small hack you figured out.

Mindfulness Exercise:

Sometimes in motherhood, you will need to "turn down the volume" on other people's opinions and advice. This is a good practice to get into now and keep in your pocket for all future challenges in parenting (and many other aspects of your life).

If you've had a negative encounter lately that left you feeling wounded, frustrated, or hopeless, you are going to meditate on what that person said. If there's no specific incident that comes to mind, you can focus on something you're sensitive about or worried that others might comment on at some point.

Mentally recall or imagine the negative feedback or warning being said, observing yourself not reacting at all. Then picture an imaginary dial in front of or on the person's face or mouth and use your hand to manually turn the volume down on what they are saying so you can no longer hear the words. Then you can picture yourself nodding, smiling, issuing a canned response or none at all, and moving right along.

The more often you practice this quick and easy meditation, the sooner you will discover yourself "turning down the volume" on naysayers and critics when you face them. And that, Mama, is when you will be free to just relax and enjoy your life and baby.

My favorite response to unsolicited advice from strangers is “Sorry, do I know you?” Works like a charm!

A Real Mama

Can I Get an ETA on "This Too Shall Pass"?

Sleep Deprivation

You are in the throes of some of the most exhausting work you've ever done, and then the tiny human at the center of it has the audacity to wake up screaming just minutes after you finally fall asleep. Hang in there, Mama, because it might seem like this sleepless life is your new normal, but it's a fleeting time and you *will* get through this.

While there is no magic wand we can wave to get you and your baby sleeping more and better, this chapter will provide tips on how to safeguard your sleep as best you can and set up your life for the next few months to accommodate the fewer zzz's you're catching. In short, this is a time when you will need to expect less sleep and accept any help you can get while making your way through it. That includes the help you give yourself by lowering expectations and taking care of your own needs in addition to your baby's.

Finding the Humor

Motherhood is full of surprises, but none will catch you off guard so swiftly as the first time your sleep-deprived, zombie-like, newborn-mama self does something absolutely ridiculous after being up half the night with the baby. Here are some real stories from other new parents to remind you that you're not alone, and provide a much-needed laugh:

> *One time after my son was born, I was helping my toddler make a bracelet, and we were eating fruit off a plate. I put a glass bead in my mouth and bit it instead of the fruit. Ouch!*

This mom proves that sometimes, even with help, we lose it a little to sleep deprivation:

> *I hired a night nurse twice a week. Of course, instead of sleeping, I sat up and watched the monitor. One night I dozed off and woke up, and was convinced she had put my baby face down in his crib. I burst open the door to his room in the middle of the night and yelled, "He needs to be on his back!" only to find her sleeping next to his crib and him sleeping on his back in his crib. Of course, that woke him up!*

Another favorite is this new parent's overflowing discovery after a rough night:

I had the night shift one time during those hazy first weeks, and the next morning when my husband went to change the baby's nappy he was like, "This nappy is reeeally full..." only to find I'd put a new nappy on her with the old, folded-up nappy still inside!

And then these hilarious moments where the most basic things were just not going as they should... These moms all have the "keys" to humor when it comes to the newborn days:

One time, I searched the whole house for my car keys and finally found them in the fridge.

The first time I went out on errands with my son, I loaded the baby and groceries in the car and could not find my keys anywhere. I dumped my bag out, looked all over, and called my husband in the middle of a work meeting to tell him I thought someone had stolen my keys... Only to find them minutes later, already in the ignition.

I made a habit of using the fob from my car keys to try and "click" open the front door. Spoiler alert: That doesn't work!

Talk to your friends if you need a laugh. Ask them for their best, most absurd stories from the newborn days. Take some time to write yours down in your journal. At the moment, it feels overwhelming, and you might wonder if you'll ever sleep again. But most parents agree that the hardest part of the newborn stage is the lack of sleep, and agree that things will turn around soon. In the meantime, the memories you're making now will be precious to you one day, even if they don't always feel that way.

At the Brink

There is a reason that forced sleep deprivation is a classic form of torture. When you don't sleep, your mental and physical faculties are not operating at or near their peak. You can feel weepy, loopy, or low. Things you normally take for granted, like driving or light exercise, may be dangerous. It's OK if you feel like all you can manage right now is to get through the day, hour by hour.

This is survival mode, Mama, and there's no shame in that. Start saying "no" to anything that seems even vaguely overwhelming. Rest whenever you are granted the opportunity. Resting can look many different ways; you don't have to force yourself to take a nap if sunlight is streaming through the windows and you can't turn your brain off. Watching something boring or relaxing on TV, meditating, or listening to quiet music in a dark room are "cheats" to feeling more rested, even if sleep won't come at odd hours or the minute the baby goes down for a nap.

Getting Help

There's a reason we're mentioning "help" in many chapters! Securing any kind of help you possibly can is going to be so important during this time. For many moms, relinquishing control is hard in the early weeks and months, but it will be key to getting through this time feeling as energized and joy-filled as possible.

Trust your partner to take care of the baby in their own way, even if they don't do things *exactly* like you do. Sit down with grandparents or sitters and go over the best practices from pace-feeding to back-sleeping, so when they do step in to watch the baby, your nerves are eased and you can truly relax.

But help comes in many forms, so even if you are not feeling quite ready to pass the baby off to someone else's arms and sleep, you can still seek it. The biggest way my husband was able to help me with my newborn sleep deprivation was by doing all the driving during his paternity leave. He took us to all our doctor's appointments, mine and Baby's, and drove me to and from any errands I needed to run, including just around town to get out of the house for a bit. I love to drive, but in the first couple of months after each baby's birth, my reflexes were slower, and I just didn't feel up to the task. If you can set up a system of drivers made up of your partner, friends, and family members, that's a great way to help buoy you at this time.

Another type of help is with the housework that plagues you. Cleaners are a worthy investment for any parent, especially sleep-deprived, brand-new ones. One cleaning session is typically the cost of two or three restaurant meals, so that's a good budgeting swap to make if you can. A less expensive but tremendous form of help is hiring someone to come by once a week and just put your clean, folded laundry away. This is something I started while pregnant with my third, and we still have it to this day. Try asking around your mom friends if they know anyone who offers this service, or inquire in a local mom's group on Facebook. The woman I hired is actually a stay-at-home mom of elementary-aged kids who charges hourly for laundry help to earn some side cash while her kids are at school. It's a win for all involved!

Of course, overnight help is solid gold, and if you're willing to let them, the people who love you want to help with this. If you're partnered, set up an on-off schedule so you are not the only one waking up overnight with the baby. Even if you're breastfeeding, they can make you feel less alone in the middle of the night by taking some of the work from you. Additionally, overnight nurses and nannies, your mom or mother-in-law, a trusted friend or neighbor, etc., are all avenues to explore.

I had a hard time passing my infants off at night to my husband as I breastfed, and they all struggled with bottles, but I happily handed them over to him in the early mornings so I could catch a few precious hours of sleep before starting the day. Another "help" you can add to your roster is to keep Baby's crib or bassinet near your bed. This makes it easier to get them and put them back when they wake at night. For my second and third babies I used a rocking bassinet that let me reach out one hand like a dramatic Hollywood starlet and gently rock the baby without getting all the way up. That bassinet was magic and, honestly, better than any human help I could've asked for!

Asking for help can be hard, especially if the first time you try, you don't get what you need. But remember these words when you're in a bind and need someone to pitch in: You deserve the guidance, wisdom, and comfort from someone who's been here before and knows what to do. There is absolutely no shame in asking; and if the first attempt falls flat, keep trying until you get what you need.

One mom shared this touching story with us about the period right after her first child's birth, when she was struggling in the hospital with endless crying and unsure what to do. 48 hours in, sleep-deprived and desperate to get her baby to settle, she rang the midwife button:

> *When [she] arrived her body language wasn't exactly friendly; she stood at the end of the bed and crossed her arms, asking what was wrong. I explained that I'd tried everything I could think of to help my baby settle and that I just didn't know what else to do. She proceeded to tell me, with what felt like very little empathy, that this was normal*

with tiny babies. I asked if she had any suggestions that I could try. She then said I should just try sitting up in bed and propping her up on my bent legs to see if she would sleep if she was in a more upright position, and then she left. Her tone of voice made me feel stupid for asking for help, and what did I think was going to happen when I had a baby?! I felt like she'd basically told me off, that she thought I was young and naïve, and that I'd obviously had a baby with no clue as to what I was undertaking. I was so desperately tired and just wanted to sleep, so I sat up in bed with the baby on my knees and quietly sobbed. Then I called my Mum, crying and whispering into the phone, as I didn't want to disturb the other lady on the ward. She was really cross that the midwife hadn't helped me and threatened to come down to the hospital, but I knew they wouldn't let her onto the ward as it was so late, so I convinced her not to, telling her I'd be fine. Just then another midwife appeared; the other lady on the ward had kindly gone and found a different midwife to help me. This midwife was all the help I needed her to be; she had a kind smile and listened sympathetically, nodding and telling me it would be ok. She then said she'd take the baby with her and settle her so that I could get some sleep! Her reaction was so completely different from that of the first midwife and exactly what I needed that I almost started crying again in relief. I woke up about an hour later with my baby tucked up beside me, fast asleep. I felt human again and was so incredibly grateful to the second midwife, who hadn't judged me but had seen my need in that moment and had met it with kindness and compassion.

Managing on Less Sleep

The fact is, you'll be sleeping less for the next little while, and you are going to have to find a way to take care of your mental and physical well-being despite this. We've already touched on taking any nap you possibly can and accepting all the help.

Mindfulness exercises like a simple breathing exercise or closing your eyes and placing your hands on your lap—palms up to receive energy or down to ground you—will help you get centered. Ease of schedule, like saying "no" to people who add stress, canceling any plan you can't manage, and tossing the housework checklist are also good.

Many moms find that hiding the clocks and deleting the baby scheduling apps are a huge help, too. Sometimes we hold ourselves to ridiculous standards and feel we need to be doing everything according to a "best plan." In the early newborn days, when you're functioning on less sleep than you've ever experienced and keeping a helpless new baby fed, clean, and thriving, the last thing you need is the stress of a set schedule.

What we're saying here is that when all the structured plans and lists fail, it's time to make like an experienced mom and just wing it!

The fact is, you will feel tired. Accept that as a truth you are observing rather than caving beneath. Cope by doing less, remembering that cocoon we've talked about building around yourself. Keep yourself as relaxed as possible while remembering that this is only a phase, and it will be over before you know it.

Stop Comparing

My best friend has been reminding me that "comparison is the thief of joy" since we were teenagers. Now that we're moms, it comes up more than ever. This is not a time when you need to be doom-scrolling on Facebook and Instagram looking at other people's posts about their perfect sleepers or 10-step morning skincare routines. You also do not need to be sitting in a group of women bragging about how easy their babies are to put down at night or for naps.

Protect yourself from information that is going to make you feel like something is wrong in your house. Nothing is wrong in your house. The norm is that babies flip-flop their days and nights for the first couple weeks or longer and still wake up many times a night for long after that point. The norm is that new mothers feel burnt out, exhausted, and overwhelmed by a lack of sleep. An exception to the norm is just a blip on the parenting radar—that mom might be experiencing great sleep, but something else will challenge her down the line.

Don't stack up your sleep schedule against anyone else's and worry that you are doing something wrong or not coping as well as others. It's a waste of your time to think like this, and as my best friend always reminds me, it steals away the joys you do have in this moment. Those are far more important to focus on than the hard parts.

Feeling Low

Losing sleep can make us feel down and blue and can be a contributing factor to an overall sense of sadness or longing for our former selves. Like we've discussed throughout the book, when you feel that way, it's important to take care of yourself emotionally. Do something you enjoy; take a walk outside in the sunshine; talk to your partner or a trusted friend or family member.

If the exhaustion becomes a source of relentless stress or sadness, reaching out to a professional can get you back on track. You're not in this alone, even though it sometimes feels this way. Most mothers in all of history have been right where you are right now, and eventually, we all started sleeping again.

Take a Mindful Minute

Journal Prompts:

- *Happy Thoughts.* Focusing on a lack of sleep or keeping a record of how often you and your baby are sleeping is not going to help you get through this time. Instead, today's journal prompts are to keep you focused on the positive:
- What was the cutest or most exciting thing your baby did today?
- If you met another mom who felt just like you do right now, what would you tell her? *(Read this one back to yourself when done.)*

Mindfulness Exercise:

The goal of this chapter's meditation is to relax you as completely as possible, bearing in mind that you are likely not getting a full and proper night's sleep at the moment. You can do this sitting on the couch or a comfortable chair, or lying down on a carpeted floor or yoga mat. Add soothing music or white noise if it helps to clear your mind of any stress. Draw the curtains and turn out the light. You can set a five- or ten-minute alarm if you're worried that you might fall asleep and don't want to! If someone else is on hand to tend to Baby, though, falling asleep at the end wouldn't be the worst thing.

Start with a cleansing breath, in through the nose and out through the mouth. Extend your exhale as long as possible so you are completely empty of air. Repeat this two or three times, while you settle your mind into relaxation mode. Picture your negative thoughts as little bubbles or balloons, and watch them float away into a clear blue sky.

Where do you feel tension in your body? Is it in your feet, in your neck, or at your temples? Scan your body for tension and discomfort, and part by part, imagine a pair of hands gently descending to massage loose the knots and stress in each part. This meditation can be as brief or long as you want and need it to be. You should emerge feeling relaxed, comforted, and ready to face the rest of your day—or night, as the case may be!

"In the midst of those first few blurry newborn weeks, sleep was almost non-existent. One day the postman knocked on the door, bleary eyed, I accepted the parcel, thanked him and told him 'bye, love you!'. I wanted the ground to open up and swallow me! At least my boobs weren't out."

A Real Mama

More Than a Mother

Rediscovering Self & Identity

Becoming a mom adds a whole new layer to your life experience and identity. It also strips away some of our former layers, leaving many of us wondering what happened to who we were before. It's normal to have an adjustment period of doubt and missing your former self, especially in the newborn days when care tasks for the baby often feel never-ending.

But your old self is in there somewhere, just with some pieces hibernating at the moment. And when you feel ready to bring your favorite parts of her back (like yoga class and dinners out with close friends), she'll be there. In the meantime, it's important to take care of the *you* that you are now and to start learning more about mom-you, who has a new perspective and is changed in ways that make you even better than you were before.

Loss of Identity

This isn't the first time in your life that you've made a big change and become someone new—there's school, job changes, moving in with a partner, and building a life together. But having a child is the most momentous shift because you're not only changing into a new version of yourself but also adding a whole new person—one who's entirely dependent on you—to the picture.

Thinking of it like that, is there any conceivable way that you *wouldn't* feel overwhelmed and wholly changed?

Taking care of a baby is an around-the-clock effort, as you're learning, and at times the exhaustion we talked about in Chapter 8 can cloak our other emotions. The defeated or deflated feelings that come alongside tiredness can make us feel like this whole mom thing is just too much, leaving us longing for who we were before.

Here's the good news: Even though you will never go back to not being a mom, all the best parts of you are still in there. The pieces of your life experience that are out of the question for this very moment live on in your memories for a reason. And many, if not all of them will be a part of your reality again one day. In the meantime, you have a whole new "you" to get to know... And she's pretty great, too.

Explore Your New Identity

So, skydiving and international travel are shelved for the moment. So what? You have a lot to offer this world, and you are just getting started. Let's talk about all the positive changes that have started to unfold since your sweet little baby hit the scene:

1. **Selfless Human Potential Unlocked.** OK, you knew you were going to love your baby, but did you know that your body was going to fight like it's never fought for anything before, to bring this person into the world? Did you know that you were going to become the kind of person who loses sleep to comfort someone else? That you'd soon be a person who can fold laundry one-handed and will weep in empathy over a tiny baby actor who is crying during a diaper change on a TV commercial? Welcome to the realm of selflessness and endless love. Welcome to being a mom.These examples are randomized and some are borderline silly, but the point here is that a new, maybe untapped, or at least heavily deepened part of you is emerging in the role of Mother. You are learning what it is to raise and support a human life from its very beginnings, and you will guide, nurture, and love this person like you have never loved anyone before, ever. That's a lot to adjust to! Be patient with yourself while riding these waves.

2. **Center of the Universe Status Secured.** There is now a person in this world who considers you True North. More than your parents and siblings who've loved you from Day One; more than your best friend who chose you and still adores you for all your quirks and attributes; more than

your partner who had this baby with you. To that little baby, you are the whole world and everything in it. As he or she grows, they will continue to look up, to look for, and to look across the room at their mother. To feel your support and guidance in every stage.

Did you know that the most common word uttered on death beds is "*Mama*"? I'm not trying to be morbid here; this is important, though, because it shows the strength and hugeness of what you have become. You are the lifelong guidepost for another human life. There is so much power and potential in this truth.

3. **A Better You.** Things are still new, and your "baby brain" might have you feeling hazy, but the best parts of momming are still to come. Many mothers report feeling that they become better communicators and listeners as they grow in this role, something that extends beyond the home to help them at work and in friendships, too. Motherhood gives you a different perspective on life, helping you stay calm in tough situations and motivating you to do better and learn more. Becoming a mother also gives a new sense of purpose and meaning that will last forever.

4. **Brain & Body Buzz.** You might have been ruminating on the emotional benefits of becoming a mom, but did you know there are proven chemical and physical benefits, too? Stud-

ies have shown that becoming a mother increases the gray matter in your brain, rendering you a better decision-maker and judge of character and situations; increasing your motivation and appreciation of rewards and joys; and making you better at processing emotions.

Motherhood also increases cardiac health, drives down your risk of stroke and certain cancers including breast and ovarian, and leads many women to make healthier choices in their diet and lifestyle, with the goal of being a good example for their kids.

For these reasons and so many more, you will love this role the more you grow into it. Right now, lean into learning who you are as a mom. Observe your personal growth and where your opinions on some issues might have shifted. This will be an evolving part of your personality as your baby grows; it might be interesting to do some journaling on it and look back in time to see it develop.

Sharing & Relating

Finding a bridge in your discussions with other moms will soften the blow of a shifting identity. It's OK to admit to a friend that you feel different and miss your old self. Make sure to listen while they share their woes, too. You are not alone in thinking wistfully of a carefree past and, of course, wishing you could get more sleep.

Experienced and brand-new moms alike can be a source of comfort and relating while you work through these feelings. And most moms who are out of the baby stage will tell you with confidence that they got back to many of their favorite hobbies eventually, and even took up new ones.

Communicate & Create Me-Time

Tell your partner or a trusted friend or family member how you feel. Sometimes, just getting it off your chest and hearing aloud the words, "I don't feel like myself!" can be cleansing. Open up to someone you can trust, and keep those lines open. If you are partnered, the other person on this parenting journey with you has to be told how you are feeling so they can help. You might be surprised to learn that they feel similarly, too.

Explain the fact that you need a little bit of time to yourself to decompress and feel human. Don't apologize for this, because it's normal and necessary. Taking short breaks will let you feel like yourself again, even if you only get away for a little while. It'll give you the time you need to remember who you were before, and it will make you that much more eager to get back to your baby and enjoy all the cuddles upon your return.

When my first child was very little and my husband was working crazy hours, my own mom insisted I hire a babysitter twice a week for a few hours. I resisted at first, but those two brief weekly breaks ended up being the best thing for me. I would take a walk, read a book, and get some grocery shopping done in peace. Often, I'd have to laugh at myself for spending a decent chunk of that time scrolling through pictures of the baby or shopping for new little outfits or toys for her while we were apart.

It doesn't matter what you do with your me-time as long as you take it. I have a friend who would hire a babysitter so she could go hide in her bedroom and take a midday nap. This is a great time to revisit a hobby or ritual you enjoyed before becoming a mom. Maybe you just want to wander the aisles of your favorite store alone or catch up with a good friend over the phone. It's basically an opportunity for much-needed self-care that comes in many forms. From face masks to retail therapy, you'll decide the day—or hour—of your me-time and what you want to do with it. Regardless, reach out for help to take a very needed and deserved break, and you'll come back feeling refreshed.

It takes a while to adjust to becoming a mom, and all the time, energy, and practicality restraints therein. While you're growing into this role, you can relish in the past while enjoying the process of getting to know who you are now. After all, you're not saying goodbye to the person you were before; you're just adding new and wonderful things to the list of what makes her special.

Take a Mindful Minute

Journal Prompt:

- *Find a bridge.* When you're deep in new-mom life, it can be hard to see what's next without mourning what came before. What are some threads that tie between the two? What activities that you have always loved can you and your baby do together? What about motherhood has reminded you of, or allowed you to slow down enough to enjoy, something you used to be more interested in? For example, for me, yoga was a big part of my life before having children. Once approved by my doctor for exercise, I started taking mommy-and-me classes. Now, yoga is something my children and I enjoy doing together. As for rediscovered joys, exploring the world of baby clothes and accessories brought out my inner fashionista, who had been hiding within.

Mindfulness Exercise:

Visualization of positives is a great tool for reclaiming joy and promoting a healthier mindset. You don't need a ton of time to make this mindfulness practice impactful. With closed eyes or a soft gaze, picture yourself doing your favorite things or seeing your favorite people—anything from which you've had a mandatory distance since giving birth.

Now imagine your child's presence there, either currently as a baby or in the future as a child or young adult. Visualizing them included might mean they are partaking in your hobby or passion with you; it may also mean you see them at home with a sitter while you are doing it. Picture your child laughing, content, and enjoying themselves there with you or not. This is the outcome of quality childcare and a break for yourself. You can apply it practically; all it takes is the first step in talking to someone who cares and making a plan to regain some of that woman who still lives within you.

Motherhood is not about losing yourself, but discovering the best version of who you are.

Final Words for the New Mama

Conclusion

You're at the start of your motherhood journey, and things will continue to become second nature and easier to manage as you go. This is a special time learning how to parent, getting to know your baby, and getting to know yourself in the role of Mother.

Hopefully this book has given you the tools to push through the harder parts of the newborn period and the first several months of your little one's life, so you can enjoy the easier and happier bits but give yourself grace when it's tough. While there is no "easy" stage of motherhood, many women find that the newborn days are among the most challenging, as there is just so much to learn and so little time.

When you are feeling low, return to our meditation and journal prompts or breeze back through the funny, real-mom moments we've shared for a quick laugh. Always take comfort in the knowledge that the hard feelings, the exhaustion, and the doubt are nothing new; these challenges are part of the universal experience of mothering young children. You will learn to live with them and work around them as Baby grows.

Take lots of photos and videos during this time, because you'll want to remember it all. Make sure to get in some of these shots as well, whether you're showered and fresh-faced or messy-haired in last night's pajamas. Make a record of your moments, good and bad. In hindsight, you'll want to pore over the traces of this time. And, if you have more children in the future, your then-self will appreciate the reminder that they've been here before!

Love is the most important thing you can give to your child. Expensive sleep sacks, custom nursery drapes, homemade baby food, and even the most state-of-the-art stroller could never rival the comfort of your touch and the soothing of your voice. Rest in the knowledge that you were hand-picked to be the mother of this wonderful child, to guide them, and to love them from the moment they burst forth from your body until you take your last breaths.

Ignore anyone who tries to take the joy of this time away. Build that cocoon we have referenced to keep yourself and your little family protected from judgment or pressure from the outside world. Say "no" to every plan that doesn't suit you. Say "yes" to every offer of help from someone you trust. Slow down and take things one day at a time.

And always, *always* take the time to care for that sweet baby's mother. Her well-being and happiness are more important now than ever before.

You’ve got this, mama.

THANK YOU!

You're the Best

Thank you for choosing *The Newborn Mama* as your companion on this incredible journey of motherhood! We hope you found the advice, reassurance, and comfort within these pages helpful as you navigate your new role as a mom.

As a special thank you we'd love to send you a free gift! We have designed a set of 16 beautiful flashcards featuring positive affirmations for the new mother. Download them from this link, or scan the QR code below to access them.

If you enjoyed the book and found it helpful, would you mind taking a moment to leave a review? Your feedback means the world to us and helps other moms find the support they need.

Wishing you all the best on your motherhood journey, and remember, you're doing an amazing job!

About the Author

Get to Know Ashley!

Ashley Tobin is a passionate writer, mother, and advocate for mindful parenting. As the author of *The Newborn Mama*, Ashley draws from her own experiences as a mother of three to provide guidance, reassurance, and support to new moms embarking on their motherhood journey.

Ashley has also authored two popular kids' activity books focused on mindfulness, helping children develop emotional intelligence and resilience from a young age.

With a deep-rooted passion for promoting positive mental health, Ashley is dedicated to creating resources that nurture both parent and child. When she's not writing, Ashley enjoys spending quality time with her family, exploring nature, and getting lost in a good book!

You can follow Ashley on Amazon, Instagram and Facebook.

ALSO BY ASHLEY TOBIN

Are you looking for a way to help your child understand and manage their emotions?

Look no further than *Emotion Detective*! This self regulation workbook for kids is designed for ages 6-14, and features the Emotion Detective, who teaches children and tweens to recognize their feelings and express them in a healthy way, developing their executive functioning skills and social emotional learning.

With a fun detective theme, your child will love filling out the daily prompts and making journaling a part of their everyday routine. This calming emotions journal teaches coping skills and mindfulness for kids to help with anxiety, stress and anger.

AVAILABLE ON AMAZON

ALSO BY ASHLEY TOBIN

Give your child mindfulness tools to help manage and understand ADHD with this calming, fun and creative activity book.

Children with ADHD can benefit greatly from practising mindfulness. Mindfulness Magic is filled with activities designed to help with focus, self-regulation, and positivity. By encouraging your child to be mindful and present, they can learn to understand their emotions, express their feelings, stay calm, and improve their concentration skills.

Mindful thinking is important for mental health, self-esteem, and confidence. By practising mindfulness exercises and feeling in control, children can learn to view their ADHD as a unique asset and harness the amazing abilities it provides them with.

AVAILABLE ON AMAZON

Printed in Dunstable, United Kingdom

66866337R00071